CW00801352

UNDER THE SURFACE - SOMERSET FLOODS

BURROWHILLBOOKS

Published in 2014
by Burrow Hill Books
Pass Vale Farm, Burrow Hill
Kingsbury Episcopi
Martock, Somerset
TA126BU
www.matildatemperley.com

Edition 1
ISBN: 978-0-9929401-0-2

A catalogue record for this book is available from the British Library

Author Matilda Temperley
Picture editor Stefano Broli
Graphic design by Priscille Neefs
Additional graphics Lara Stower

Printed and bound by
EBS - Editoriale Bortolazzi Stei srl
Via Monte Comun 40
37057 San Giovanni Lupatoto
Verona - Italy

UNDER THE SURFACE - SOMERSET FLOODS

Matilda Temperley

MATILDA TEMPERLEY

FOREWORD

MICHAEL EAVIS

The founder of Glastonbury Festival

My family have been dairy farmers in Somerset for generations and like other local farmers we are familiar with the problems of farming on the Levels. The fields have rhynes instead of fences and the drainage system is never far from our thoughts. The landscape supports huge biodiversity and the wildlife happily coexists with working farms. In my view it is an ecosystem that we should both celebrate and treasure.

The flooding of the past two winters has caused havoc for the people who live in the vicinity of the rivers Parrett, Brue and Tone. After the floods of 2012/13 we were told it was a 'once in a 100 year event.' Unfortunately this year, 2014, it all happened again and it was a lot deeper and lasted a lot longer. The fact that the rivers haven't been cleaned for 20 years and can only carry 58% of the water they should to the sea, means that the other 42% floods the land and villages. To me it's that simple.

Three thousand years ago, the levels were covered by sea and Glastonbury was a regular port of call for Phoenician traders. Legend says Joseph of Arimathea came here to buy lead and copper and brought Christianity with him.

Eventually the Abbey was built and the monks continued draining the land. The work they started continued up to 20 years ago when the Environment Agency decided it was no longer worth maintaining the rivers and put their very selective ideas about what sort environment they wanted before common sense.

These photographs are an important historical record of the human and environmental cost of neglecting a complex system that evolved over centuries. For the sake of the meadows, the wild flowers and the fields and farmers and the cows, this drainage has to be done. There's no other way.

INTRODUCTION

As members of the Bradford clan, we arrived in the parish of Kingsbury Episcopi in Somerset in the 16th century. Our family history is intrinsically linked to that of River Parrett. My forefathers settled in Thorney and the neighbouring Parrett was put to use while they established themselves as coal and agricultural merchants, running barges from South Wales up the river to Thorney and beyond. The firm is still a builder's merchants today.

My 99-year-old grandfather lives in Thorney. He was a physics professor and is now a flood refugee waiting to move back into the ancestral home, which before last year flooded only once, back in 1928.

To me the Levels have always been a dream landscape of rhynes and meadows full of wildlife. It is flat, fertile land that is peppered with willow trees and criss-crossed by a thousand miles of drainage ditches. These are expertly maintained by those who tend the land; farmers, withy growers, basket makers and smallholders.

The Somerset Levels, like much of natural England, are sculpted by man's efforts. The Neolithic people were amongst the first to exploit the Somerset Levels and circa 3800BC built the Sweet Track, one of the first known wooden walkways across what was then reed swamps. Later the Romans swept through and the reclamation of this marshland began with the expansion of the river system. A millennia old, man-managed drainage system was born, facilitating the romance and legends of the Somerset Levels. In the Middle Ages the responsibility of its expansion became the remit of the surrounding monasteries of Glastonbury, Athelney and Muchelney.

By the 19th century pumping stations were being built to further regulate the winter floods. Maintenance of this fragile and unique ecosystem was deemed important enough that during the Second World War Italian prisoners of war were deployed to dredge the waterways.

However, in 1996 the management of our waterways was taken over by the Environmental Agency. Their first act was to abandon the timeless policy of dredging and sell off or break up the machinery required for the task. The River Parrett that once could take a 60ft barge is now barely navigable by a canoe during the summer months. As the only route to the sea, this leisurely river is running at less than 60% of the capacity it was during the 1960s, as it is now sadly blocked by years of undredged silt. It is therefore of little surprise to the farmers of the Levels that our floods have been escalating disproportionately to the rainfall during these years of neglect. Unusual summer floods have led to stagnating ponds of toxic water, decimating the flora and fauna of the Levels and killing its wildlife.

In the winter of 2012/2013 we faced the worst floods in living memory. We expect floods to affect our farmland during the winter but homes across the Levels are built on the 'neys' or ancient islands. In 2012, and for the first time since they were built, houses were flooded and the residents called for 20 years of neglected river maintenance to be addressed.

This year saw what was described in 2013 as a 'once in a century event' happen again, only this time the water was deeper and the flooding lasted longer. The relevant agencies' own data showed us that if the river had been cleared, as it had been historically, the disruption to people's lives, the damage to the local economy, as well as the consequences to farming and the environment would have been vastly less severe.

By January 2nd 2014, homes which had escaped the floods of 2012 were inundated by the floodwater and evacuated. These are not ill-placed new builds, but houses that date back to the 17th century. By the end of January on top of what were already unprecedented floods, we suffered unusually heavy rain and the villages of Fordgate and Moorland went under.

After being submerged for up to two months homes needed to be re-plastered, refloored, rewired, refurnished and the white goods replaced. The story is the same in each home, farm and business. Even those not overtaken by the waters had access routes cut off and were forced to take lengthy, circuitous routes to work or school. In Muchelney residents had to use a water taxi along what had been the main road for months. Farmers lost land, homes, barns, crops, fodder, machinery and in some cases their livelihoods.

During the height of the flooding, we had to listen to the Environment Agency and in particular its chairman, Lord Smith of Finsbury, disputing the logic of dredging, all the while ignoring their own data. Finally, the Prime Minister stood up in the House of Commons and ordered them to dredge the River Parrett, declaring that money was no object.

By not dredging, the EA had hoped to encourage wildlife. This was a 'just add water' attitude dreamt up by their previous chairman Baroness Young. However, for the second year running this attitude has led to a vast stagnating inland sea filled with drowned villages, farms, rotting animal carcasses and sewage. A staggering 65 square miles of land was underwater. Ironically, much of the wildlife that the EA had hoped to encourage had now drowned or fled.

The floods of 2014 brought with them an extraordinary community uprising. Looking at more destruction and acutely aware of the failed promises of effective dredging in 2013 there was a revolt from the local people of the Levels.

The King Alfred Inn at Burrowbridge became a hub for action for volunteers and the media. Press releases were signed off and disseminated and journalists harangued. At one stage, after a disappointing report from Panorama, the BBC were banned from the pub and therefore from access to the epicentre of the flooding story. Social media began to play a huge role in uniting those afflicted and people from across the country came to donate services and time.

The newly discovered activism is still gaining pace in the form of the Flooding on the Levels Action Group (FLAG), formed by members of the community. This group has challenged the Environment Agency's response to the floods and questions the commitment of the agency to fulfill its promises. In Somerset we had found a voice and after two years of flooding we had learnt that those responsible for our rivers must be held to account immediately to prevent another catastrophe.

This whole unfortunate and avoidable episode has seen a huge rise in rhetoric about how to protect the Levels in the future, with big schemes and grand ideas being mooted. For many these serve as red herrings that distract us from the simple fact that a millennia old waterway system has been neglected and mismanaged by the agencies who were responsible for it. All the while the expertise of generations of farmers and landowners has been largely ignored. We cannot escape the fact that in order to safeguard our future we must look to the past.

MATILDA TEMPERLEY

A FLOOD HISTORY

Bunds, berms, holding ponds, SuDS law, urban runoff, maize runoff, mole drains, sub-soiling, sandbags, spillways, syphons, pumping stations, barrages, clyses, sluices, tidal lagoons; all are in the melting pot, including the Environment Agency which has got itself into a right pickle.

It is only when you walk the floods and talk to people and see their flooded homes that you realise the true scale of the devastation. Many farmers were forced out of their farms. Cattle, sheep, horses and chickens evacuated to higher ground. The only waders to be seen were those that come up to your chest, as Nigel Farage discovered. One might have thought he was acting as a male model for some fishing magazine. A deluge of other politicians also piled in, but piling in Somerset usually means beefing up the river banks that are in danger of slipping, and if the banks give way floods can be catastrophic. The sudden media feeding frenzy highlighted the fact that floods are as much a political and administrative problem as a natural disaster. At least the Internal Drainage Boards are made up of local farmers who know Somerset like the backs of their hands.

But flooding is endemic. For thousands of years much of Somerset was an untamed wetland of 'fenne, stagne and marishe' : peat moors and meres penned in by coastal dunes and sea walls dating back to Roman and Saxon times. Over the last 800 years wetland was slowly drained inch by inch and brought into agricultural production, first by abbeys and then by farmers prepared to dig deep into their pockets. Many of the banks like Beer Wall, Lake Wall, Stanmoor, Burrow and Baltmoor Wall are medieval and by channelling the river the monks began a process which has continued to this day. But with two very wet winters in a row things are slipping back into the mire. Is it just the weather and geography or has something else gone wrong?

Somerset or Sumorsaete, means 'summer settlers' who moved onto the rich grazing with cattle, sheep and geese, which would then be taken off and sold in the autumn. Cattle which also came from Devon, Wales and Ireland to be fattened up. Rich pastures that every year gave abundant milk for hundreds of tons of Cheddar cheese. But sudden floods can be fatal. In 1607 a tidal surge drove the sea as far inland as Glastonbury Tor. Thirty villages in Somerset were swamped and 300 people were drowned as well as livestock. In 1703 another great storm hit Somerset and hundreds more were drowned. Daniel Defoe wrote an account called The Storm which was published in 1704. It is still regarded as a pioneering work of modern journalism.

The worst flood of the 20th century was when the Tone burst its banks at Athelney on Remembrance Day, 11th November 1929, and water stayed on the land till February 1930. In three months 812 mm of rain fell. Many retreated upstairs with jugs of cider and rowing boats were tied to bedroom windows. The 1 in 100 year flood the Environment Agency should have planned for.

The years 1951 and 1960 where also bad and Taunton market flooded. In Langport people still talk of driving cattle up to their chests in water along Bow Street to get them to the railway station. Modern pumping stations were built and diesel engines switched to electric.

Geography also plays a large part in the flooding equation. It is the inland moors where the majority of the flooding occurs, but it is the Somerset Levels, technically the higher coastal clay belt, which dams the whole catchment area in. It is through this clay belt that the Parrett has to flow. Then it meets surges, bores and the general cantankerousness of the Bristol Channel, which, with a springer on and good north-westerly, can put four feet on top of a tide which pens the Parrett in for days, thus forcing the excess water over the banks into the low lying farmland and villages where it stays for weeks, even months.

To complicate matters further the Parrett is not just one river, it is six or even seven rivers, if you add Sowy, Cary and King's Sedgemoor Drain to the Tone, Isle and Yeo. There is the Brue and Huntspill both of which, like the K.S.D., have tidal clyses. The main bottle necks being Langport and Burrowbridge. The Axe, Yeo and Blind Yeo to the north have also been tamed by tidal clyses and flooding is no longer a real problem, but they have much smaller catchment areas. The Parrett Catchment area is nearly twice the size of Dartmoor. Size matters.

Contrary to common opinion the Dutch did not drain the Levels as they had drained the Fens. Cornelius Vermuyden came down in 1633 and drew up plans but they were not implemented for over 150 years. In a strange reversal of roles it was the local people who objected. They could see that drainage would lead to dispossession of their ancient common grazing rights. Even as late as 1775 William Fairchild attempted to survey King's Sedgemoor and was met by 100 villagers who chased him away, saying he would 'meet damage'. Someone dug his grave and a hogshead of cider was offered to the man who caught him. This was Somerset after all.

For many farmers the obvious solution is river dredging, which the Environment Agency, backed to the hilt by Natural England, the RSPB and a shed load of EU regulations, effectively banned for the last eighteen years. The E.A. even threatened to prosecute anyone who dredged. Was there a hidden agenda? Combine this non-dredging policy with Baroness Young's statement in 2005 that she would 'like to attach limpet mines to every pumping station in Somerset' and ' Lets add water' attitude you have a recipe for disaster. In the old days people blamed God for floods. Now they blame the Environment Agency. Spot the difference.

Dredging, however, is not the whole answer, but it does maintain river profiles and localised drainage which keeps the land in fine and productive fettle. To ignore the advice of Internal Drainage Boards and let rivers become choked with silt so that they only function at 60% of their capacity is a serious error, bordering on criminal negligence. Too many chiefs and not enough highly skilled dragline dredger men. Bring back the Court of Sewers!

It needs men of action like Brunel who in 1841 devised the world's first steam driven dredger-cum-scraper to shift the silt from Bridgwater docks. She was called Bertha and weighed in at sixty tons and still exists. Dredging also involved Ruston Bucyrus dragline excavators and 21 of these were used by the National Rivers Authority until about 1996 when the Environment Agency took over and sold them off.
Silt agitation is another method. The Pioneer and Eroder were well known vessels in use on the Parrett with powerful hoses, dislodging tidal silt sending it on its way back downstream to Coleridge's sunless sea.

Pleading poverty is no defence. The E.A. has just completed a very fine flood defence project and bird reserve at Steart at the Parrett's Mouth which cost c £21 Million, though £10 Million came from Port of Bristol Authority. Dredging the Parrett effectively would only cost only £4-£5 Million. Peanuts.

The other option is a tidal clyse or barrage, to keep the high tides and estuarine silt at bay.
Indeed Vermuyden first came up with the idea in the Fens and the famous Denver sluice was originally built by him in 1651. Nearly 300 years later in 1941 the Somerset Rivers Catchment Board were still debating the issue. Extensive modelling and trials were conducted and a barrage was recommended two miles above Bridgwater with an alternative site at Dunball, but slime batches and navigation killed that idea off. Slime batches were landing stages just above and below Bridgwater where silt was gathered to make Bath Bricks, used for scouring, cleaning and polishing, even sharpening knives and went all over the empire. And then there is the question of eels and elvers who love to migrate up and down the Parrett. Have they been consulted I wonder? Do they have a vote? Are the elver men an endangered species?

As always it is a complex equation juggling conservation, bird watching and farming, but one thing is certain, you can't sit in an office hundreds of miles away and dredge with a computer mouse. What a drag.

JAMES CROWDEN,
author of In Time of Flood examines the history of floods and drainage on the Somerset Levels and Moors.
By kind permission of NFU Farmer and Grower Magazine 2014

1996 - The National Rivers Authority is abolished and its responsibilities absorbed by the new fangled Environment Agency. Dredging of the Somerset Levels is abandoned.

2012 - 2013 Somerset Levels have worst floods in living memory

26TH FEBRUARY 2013 - A letter from the Somerset Drainage Board Consortium
"The Environment Agency has now accepted that dredging - in the sense of de-silting and re-profiling - would make a very significant difference to the duration of flood events, and thus to their impact on people, property, agriculture and the environment. EA investigations in the wake of the 2012 flooding have shown that the capacity of the River Tone (from Hook Bridge spillway to the confluence with the River Parrett) and of the River Parrett (from the confluence with the Tone to North Moor Pumping Station) has been reduced by siltation to only around 65% of the capacity as designed in the 1960 Tone Valley Scheme. EA computer modelling has demonstrated that restoring the capacity of these two lengths of river to 85-90% of their 1960 design would "significantly reduce the duration and depth of flooding in Curry, Hay, Salt and North Moors, based on the 2012 floods"

30TH NOVEMBER 2012 - Lord Smith, Chairman of the Environment Agency, declares that he would like to see something done about the flooding in the next 6 months while on top of Burrow Mump. It is estimated that only 10 hours of dredging are carried out as a result.

3RD DECEMBER 2012 - Flooding on the Levels Action Group (FLAG) established to campaign for better water management on the Levels

14TH FEBRUARY 2013 - FLAG launches the Stop the Flooding - Dredge the Rivers campaign

16TH DECEMBER 2013 - The Environment Agency asked to pump Northmoor by local farmers but nothing happens

21ST DECEMBER 2013 - Sheep evacuated from Thorney Moor

31ST DECEMBER 2013 - The A361 floods and is closed at Burrowbridge for the next three and a half months

2ND JANUARY 2014 - Houses in Thorney and the Gray's racing yard in Moorland flood

3RD JANUARY 2014 - Muchelney cut off by flood water and accessible only by tractor or boat

27TH JANUARY 2014 - Secretary of State for the Environment, Owen Paterson visits Northmoor Pumping Station without his wellington boots

4TH FEBRUARY 2014 - Prince Charles visits Stoke St Gregory and Muchleney

5TH FEBRUARY 2014 - Villagers in Fordgate and Moorland told to evacuate by police helicopter

5TH-7TH FEBRUARY 2014 - More than 1000 cattle evacuated from the Moorland area

7TH FEBRUARY 2014 - David Cameron makes first visit to the Somerset Levels

15TH FEBRUARY 2014 - Dutch pumps start work at Dunball removing up to 15 tonnes of water per second

20TH FEBRUARY 2014 - David Cameron announces in Parliament that the River Parrett will be dredged and money is "no object"

MARCH 2014 - Flood water recedes and the clean up operation begins

14TH MARCH 2014 - The A361 reopens

24TH MARCH 2014 - Cattle begin to return to West Yeo Farm, Moorland

“In the old days people blamed God for floods. Now they blame the Environment Agency.”

JAMES CROWDEN

11TH JANUARY 2014

PREVIOUS PAGE: MARY TEMPERLEY AND RUFUS, THORNEY, 12TH JANUARY 2014
ABOVE: RUFUS, PHOENIX AND FOX, 11TH JANUARY 2014
OVERLEAF: HENRY TEMPERLEY AND BUDDY, HAMBRIDGE, 12TH JANUARY 2014

LEFT: JULIAN TEMPERLEY, THORNEY, 14TH JANUARY 2014
OVERLEAF: BARNS IN MUCHELNEY, 15TH JANUARY 2014
OVERLEAF: HUMPBACK BRIDGE HAMBRIDGE, 15TH JANUARY 2014
OVERLEAF: SEAT TOLEDO ABANDONED IN MUCHELNEY, 14TH JANUARY 2014

"My 99 year old father was evacuated from his family home on January the 1st. It will be at least a year before he can return. This was a man made disaster. We were flooded to an unprecedented level for 6 weeks before any unusually high rainfall. The only thing God can be blamed for is not giving the environment agency any brains."

JULIAN TEMPERLEY, Cider Farmer, January 2014

PREVIOUS PAGE: THE MAN MADE BANKS OF THE RIVER PARRETT EMERGING FROM THE FLOODS, 18TH FEBRUARY 2014. THE RIVER BANKS HAVE BEEN RAISED SINCE MEDIEVAL TIMES

"A heresy has been allowed to grow up that the rivers and drainage channels are ecological sites in their own right. They're not, they are largely human constructs. This is a man-made landscape. What is precious is the land and the habitat between them."

DAVID HEATH, MP The Observer 14th February 2014

RIGHT: CHRISTINE GRAY SURVEYS HER FLOODED HOUSE 13TH JANUARY 2014

"Absolute nightmare, like a horror story slowly coming true. Everytime you go to bed you are wondering how much closer water is getting, should you get out? Will it get close enough? Have you got to move everything? Can we stay here? You are on absolute tenterhooks, your stomach is in a tight knot the whole time"

CHRISTINE GRAY, ITV News 4th March 2014

LEFT: HENRY TEMPERLEY IN THORNEY, 17TH JANUARY 2014
ABOVE: THE BROWNS IN THORNEY, 17TH JANUARY 2014

"We were at home and watching with trepidation as water levels on the moors rose – and that night we saw water creeping in through crevices and cracks. People here were sand-bagging – but you can't sand-bag against this sort of creeping water torture, only against a flash flood. The water here doesn't get away quick enough. If I had a house in the middle of the moors I might expect to flood, but places like Thorney and Muchelney were called 'ney' because they were islands. This house hasn't been flooded since it was built 100 years ago."

RODDY BAILLIE-GROHMAN Western Morning News 4th March 2014

RIGHT: MICHAEL BROWN AT HOME,
17TH JANUARY 2014
OVERLEAF: THORNEY HOUSE,
21ST JANUARY 2014

"This has been an extraordinary flood. We've seen floods around us over the years and become blasé. The water would come into the garden but we've got pumps, so we always survived. But this year we pumped and it totally overwhelmed us."

MICHAEL BROWN,
Western Morning News 18th January 2014

PREVIOUS PAGE: NICK FROST'S HOUSE, THORNEY, 21ST JANUARY 2014
RIGHT: SOMERSET CIDER BRANDY BOND, THORNEY, 17TH JANUARY 2014

"Homes are uninhabitable, farms are unworkable and jobs are being expensively destroyed. On the Somerset Levels, people are scared and angry – very angry."

IAN LIDDELL-GRAINGER MP
The Guardian 24th January 2014

V510·2
V484·8
B-X95

ABOVE: A GREENHOUSE IN MUCHELNEY, 14TH JANUARY 2014
RIGHT: FLOODED WITHY BED, BURROWBRIDGE, 19TH FEBRUARY 2014

"You might think that I have a lot to say about flooding but I don't. I struggle to find anything sensible to say. My memories of those 8 weeks are strangely limited but two words come to mind - Toil and Strife! Everything was hard work, everything was in the wrong place, everything seemed vulnerable and you could do absolutely nothing about it. We were completely helpless in the presence of such overpowering forces."

DR PETER NIGHTINGALE, May 2014

LEFT: MUCHELNEY, 14TH JANUARY 2014

"Until last year I thought you brushed the water out and that was the end of it. I had no idea that your house has to be completely stripped out. I don't think people realise the devastation goes on for months."

DR LIZ NIGHTINGALE,
BBC NEWS 30th January 2014

ABOVE: MUCHELNEY AS AN ISLAND, 18TH FEBRUARY 2014

"Our island life began on Friday the 3rd of January. By Saturday, the homes that had been flooded the previous year were flooded again and the rain was still falling. The flood waters even divided the village of Muchelney into 2 or 3 smaller separate islands, and contact with some of our neighbours, let alone the outside world, became suddenly extremely difficult."

SARAH NICHOLAS, May 2014

ABOVE: FIRE SERVICE TAXI BOAT, MUCHELNEY, 18TH FEBRUARY 2014

"It is a real nightmare – everybody is really tired and morale is quite low in the village – it just feels like nobody is doing anything. The village has been cut off since New Year with all four roads in and out of the community submerged.The only way in is either on the back of a trailer towed by a tractor or boarding the emergency boat run by the fire service."

PETER HERB, Western Morning News 1st February 2014

Wizard

PREVIOUS PAGE: BOATING IN THE FLOODS, 19TH JANUARY 2014
LEFT: WAVES IN THE ROAD, 4TH FEBRUARY 2014
ABOVE: THE PRINCE OF WALES IN MUCHELNEY, 4TH FEBRUARY 2014

"There is nothing like a jolly good disaster to get people to start doing something. The tragedy is that nothing happened for so long"

PRINCE CHARLES, Muchelney 4th February 2014

On the 2nd of February I posted the following on Facebook: *"OK – so the water is coming up really fast tonight – our neighbours are flooding now and I have a nasty feeling we might go under this year – might have to call on some of you to help move/house the following...500 cows, 1 horse, 4 chickens, 2 cats, 2 dogs, 1 severely disabled elderly gentlemen + lovely wife (cooks well), 1 petulant 9 year old, 2 semi continent 4 year olds, 1 grumpy farmer and lovely wife (cooks badly) and maybe a few suitcases..."*

Then came the call from the EA, a wall of water was coming our way and there was nothing they could do to stop it. I remember the phone call from James vividly - "You have to get out, get the horse out, get the chickens out and get the kids out." Friends and neighbours came over to help me put the furniture on blocks and take treasured possessions upstairs, frantically throwing random possessions into a few suitcases. A horsebox appeared and Bert was magically whisked away. The chicken rescue squad appeared late afternoon. I only just managed to drive the children out in a 4 x 4.

James meanwhile had been frantically building banks around the sheds, but as the day wore on and the relentless rising of the water continued it became clear that the unthinkable was happening, he would have to evacuate 550 cattle.

We managed a couple of hours sleep that night in our temporary house, but woke in the early hours worrying about the practicalities of this huge undertaking; cattle movements that legally had to be logged on the computer? TB testing? And the biggie - even if we managed to get them out, where were they going to go and how on earth would we feed them? I rather flippantly said, "Don't worry – you get them out and I'll feed them!" The phone began ringing at 5.30am and so started the day from hell.

Someone had told me that Twitter was an incredibly powerful medium and so it proved that day – I sent a few tweets to the movers and shakers in the farming world and that was the beginning of an incredible effort from British farmers who understood the enormity of the task we were facing. Forage Aid (mark 2) #somerset floods was born.

Back at the farm 14 tractors and trailers came to assist in the cattle evacuation– the water was too deep for ordinary lorries, so a few cattle were loaded each time and the convoy moved off painfully slowly to travel the 5 miles to market. It was incredibly treacherous – the sides of the road were not visible and it was easy to tip the load if you got it wrong. All of those involved in the evacuation actually risked life and limb to save those animals. The move was so incredibly stressful on the cattle and no decent livestock farmer wants to see this, but the water was rising and there was no choice. By the end of that day it was chest deep in places. The next day the only way in or out of the farm was by boat over a mile of water. There were 3 convoys that day moving 400 head of cattle – a heroic effort given the circumstances. We received no help from the authorities apart from a shabby police escort arranged late in the day.

That day it became clear the neighbouring farms needed evacuating as well – although James was mentally, physically and emotionally exhausted from evacuating his own livestock, he went out there and joined the convoy – two of his tractors were written off in this effort. The final twist in the tale is that we were told that one of us NEEDED to attend a meeting in Bridgwater – James went stinking of cattle, covered in muck, wet through mid evacuation to find it was with David Cameron - I would really like to have seen that meeting!

The main challenge now the cattle are back is to rebuild. We can throw time and money into regenerating the land and repair our houses but the guarantee of a future without devastating flooding still seems shaky. The dredging is welcome but to make the area more flood resilient requires serious investment into outdated pumping stations, and some thought of how to fund the ongoing maintenance. Until I see that I will always be slightly nervous when the rain starts to fall.

JENNY WINSLADE, May 11th 2014

PREVIOUS PAGE: JAMES WINSLADE, WEST YEO FARM, 13TH JANUARY 2014
LEFT: MIKE CURTIS ORGANISING TRANSPORT, 6TH FEBRUARY 2014
ABOVE: A FULL CATTLE TRAILER IN THE DITCH, 6TH FEBRUARY 2014

"I am in a big New Holland tractor and the water is sloshing around the engine. It's about 1.5m high. It's literally like driving through the sea, it's unbelievable. We've got fleets of tractors and trailers all working to get the cows out"

GAVIN SADLER, The Farmer's Guardian 7th February 2014

Approved Livestock Market
Part of the Red Tractor Assurance chain
gth
Greenslade Taylor Hu
PAYMENT TERMS AND CONDITIONS
RETENTION OF TITLE CLAUSE

PREVIOUS PAGE: ONE OF THE EVACUEES, 6TH FEBRUARY 2014
LEFT: ROBERT VENNER SELLING JAMES'S EVACUATED CATTLE AT SEDGEMOOR MARKET, 10TH FEBRUARY 2014
OVERLEAF: DEAD BIRD LANGPORT, 4TH FEBRUARY 2014

"This is breaking James's heart. But we will fight every last breath to continue farming on the levels"

JENNY WINSLADE, Farming Today 10th February 2014

ABOVE: JANET AND RAYMOND WINSLADE'S HOUSE MOORLAND, 28TH JANUARY 2014, 12 PM

ABOVE: JANET AND RAYMOND WINSLADE'S HOUSE MOORLAND, 11TH FEBRUARY 2014, 4 PM

RIGHT: WEST YEO FARM, 18TH FEBRUARY 2014
ABOVE: JAMES WINSLADE AND JONO DIXON VISIT THE FARM 11TH FEBRUARY 2014

"The initial evacuation is the most emotional, seeing your livelihood and all that you have worked for destroyed. After you just deal with it day by day. Boat trips are surreal, a mile of open water and then wading through your home and business in waist high water. The waves even knocked our kitchen walls down" JAMES WINSLADE, May 2014

"I distinctly remember the fits of laughter when James appeared from the farmhouse carrying his filing cabinet and muttering to us 'the bloody inland revenue still need paying.' So our journey back across the fields of West Yeo Farm began, with a spluttering outboard and a howling wind we set a course for Burrow Mump." JONO DIXON, May 2014

PREVIOUS PAGE: STABLES WEST YEO FARM, 6TH FEBRUARY 2014
LEFT: GARDEN FURNITURE IN MOORLAND, 11TH FEBRUARY 2014
OVERLEAF: BURROWBRIDGE FROM THE A361, JANUARY 13TH 2014

"Before we flooded I was up every hour looking at the water. Now I stay in, pick up a large gin and tonic and go to bed. It is intimidating. We have got no heating and it's very cold. For a couple more days we will stay but I think it will be overwhelming by then. The water pumps are no longer doing any good - it's coming in again just as fast as it's being pumped out - but I don't want to leave. I'm worried about looting."

PAT MENNIM East Lyng 12th February 2014

TOP: NEIL CRADDOCK ON HIS BUND BEFORE IT WAS BREACHED, 13TH JANUARY 2014
LEFT AND ABOVE: THE WOODYARD AFTER THE BUND WAS BREACHED, 18TH FEBRUARY 2014

"The water was ten-foot deep in the factory, you can see the watermark. It's a mangled mess of wood, machinery and debris. People talk about floods, but until you see the actual devastation you don't really understand. We've been numbed by the experience, it's unbelievable. I don't think anyone can really prepare for what's happened. The bill here is close to one million and because of the floods last year we have had all insurance cover taken away."

NEIL CRADDOCK, 18th February 2014

RIGHT: BURROWBRIDGE, 20TH FEBRUARY 2014
OVERLEAF: THE OLD BASKET CENTRE ON THE A361, 20TH FEBRUARY 2014

"It's rising like hell and this water is toxic. It's full of sewage, heating oil, dead animals. I feel volunteers here are risking their health working in it. But we have no choice. Nobody else is doing it"

TIM HOLMES, The Guardian 14th February 2014

320·4T

LEFT: SAM NOTARO'S HOUSE AND BUND, MOORLAND, 18TH FEBRUARY 2014

"There were other times when I said 'bloody hell, it's coming over' and on one occasion the bank gave way, but fortunately we were able to pump the water out while it was being rebuilt. It is going to be difficult to feel secure living here knowing it could happen again."

SAM NOTARO, The Times 27th February 2014

PREVIOUS PAGE: MOORLAND, 18TH FEBRUARY 2014
RIGHT: MOORLAND CHURCH, 21ST FEBRUARY 2014
OVERLEAF: FLOATING BIBLE, 21ST FEBRUARY 2014

"There will be plenty of arguments about how the events of this year can't be allowed to happen again and politicians and others have promised you much. You are the resurrection community who must hold them to account."

RT REV PETER MAURICE,
Bishop of Taunton, 21st April 2014

RIGHT: MOORLAND, 10TH FEBRUARY 2014

"Every so often as a priest you get the feeling you have seen most things in life and then something happens that you would never have imagined. Such a day was the 7th February when we lost a whole village. "

REV JANE HASLAM, May 2014

IN
LOVING

RIGHT: THORNEY, 13TH FEBRUARY 2014
OVERLEAF: THORNEY HOUSE, 13TH FEBRUARY 2014

"As I stood on Hook Bridge at Curry Moor in early February, the drove had disappeared and the footpath was submerged. A day later the devastation struck in Moorland and life suddenly changed! We were now dealing with people's lives not only farmers livelihoods."

HEATHER VENN, Farmer, May 2014

"I went back to my house yesterday and I just couldn't get there. The water was up to my waist and I just couldn't get there. Walking away from our house was heart breaking. It's not easy walking away from everything you've ever worked for."

JULIE SHOVEL, February 5th 2014

"It felt like we were going in to clear a deceased person's home, yet in the presence of grieving relatives. In the first few weeks what stuck me most was the eerie silence, the absence of birds and wildlife and villagers and just being overwhelmed by the complete devastation that surrounded us"

LORRI BEE, FLAG Volunteer, May 2014

THORNEY WEST
FARM

TENA
75 08 30-02 SK
XL
Men
Co. Ma

ABOVE: MOORLAND, 21ST FEBRUARY 2014

ABOVE: MOORLAND, 21ST FEBRUARY 2014

RIGHT: FIRE ENGINE RESCUE IN BURROWBRIDGE, 11TH FEBRUARY 2014
OVERLEAF: THE A361 FROM BURROWBRIDGE, 26TH FEBRUARY 2014

"We may be local farmers and understand the river but us river workers, as an old boss used to tell us, are only employed from the neck down."

ANONYMOUS, EA River Worker February 2014

Weak bridge
at Huntworth
26T
mgw
Village
hall

NORDIC LOCK
PROS

HESCO
www.hesco.com

PREVIOUS PAGE: VOLUNTEERS IN MOORLAND, 21ST FEBRUARY 2014
OVERLEAF: THE OLD BASKET WORKS ON THE A361, 19TH FEBRUARY 2014
LEFT: RAVI SINGH, BURROWBRIDGE, 13TH FEBRUARY 2014

"On 7th Feb 2014 I heard callers from Somerset on the radio, they were in a distressed state and asked why the British based international relief organisations had not responded to the floods. I personally felt ashamed that Khalsa Aid was also guilty of such neglect of our own countrymen. The next day we arrived in Burrowbridge slightly nervous because we were unsure of our reception as Sikhs.

In my 15 years of relief work around the globe I have never known such a warm and welcoming community. The "official" response was disappointing, thank god for FLAG volunteers who rose like a pride of lions.

Maybe because the villages and fields of Somerset remind me of my childhood in Panjab or maybe it's due to something spiritual which has entered my soul during the floods relief, I definitely have a deep pull towards Burrowbridge and surrounding villages. The community has truly stolen my heart.

I cannot return as freely as I wish to my village in Panjab due to my political view points against the Indian government but I will surely return as much as I can to beautiful Burrowbridge. Out of the floods rose a spirit of humanity and hope. We have dredged all barriers.

Watch out for a turbaned guy walking past your homes soon... You have been warned..."

RAVI SINGH, Khalsa Aid, 12th May 2014

“Oh we made a mistake, there’s no doubt about that, and we perhaps have relied too much on the Environment Agency’s advice. I think we recognise now what we should have done… we should have dredged.”

“Well I’ll apologise. I’ll apologise unreservedly and I’m really sorry that we took the advice on what we thought we were dealing with experts.”

“I don’t think it was a question of money in the Somerset Levels. It was policy and it was a policy not to dredge and the more we know about it the more we know it was a wrong-headed decision. It’s now accepted even by the Environment Agency that was a mistake and we made a grave error.”

ERIC PICKLES, Communities Secretary, The Andrew Marr Show 9th February 2014

"Did you see any evidence of the merest scintilla of remorse or regret for the devastation the Environment Agency has been party to causing on the Somerset Levels? Because I didn't. I saw a man who made much of the fact that the Environment Agency had saved more than a million people from flooding. What does he want? A medal? That is what the Environment Agency is supposed to do. That is what Lord Smith and the senior managers are paid over-handsomely to ensure happens. Lord Smith's agency has quietly re-written the rules, designated farmland as 'reservoirs' and decided to abandon practices which have kept the Levels dry and workable for a thousand years"

IAN LIDDELL-GRAINGER MP, Mail Online 10th Feburary 2014

A BIBLICAL TALE

CHRIS RUNDLE 2014

There was, really, no other word for it: as he arrived by helicopter in Somerset at the week-end the Prime Minister was obliged to describe the devastation he had seen by falling back on that much overworked-adjective 'biblical'. As indeed it was...

And behold the rains fell without ceasing for forty days and forty nights. And the waters rose and covered the face of the earth.

And the keepers of beasts and tillers of the fields cried out in their despair, for their lands upon the plains were flooded, yea even unto the mountains in every direction.

Then they said: Where is the Lord Smith, he who is charged with keeping the waters at bay so that our cattle may graze and our crops may grow ?

And they called out to him to come and witness their misery. And he came not.

Then blew a mighty wind and came a great storm. And the waters rose higher, yea into the houses of the people, the stores wherein their grain was kept, and the byres of their beasts.

And they called out again to the Lord Smith, that he come to behold their suffering. And he came not.

Then his advisors entered into the place of Lord Smith, saying: Lord, lord, we hear the cries of the keepers of beasts and the tillers of the fields. They are sore distressed. The Prince, he that is called Charles, hath visited them bearing gifts of jam and biscuits. Shouldst thou not also travel thence to meet them?

And Lord Smith said: What care I for such men? For behold they have the straw of the fields in their ears and they hear no wisdom. Yet shall I now go and visit them that they may then remain quiet. I can just fit it in before dinner.

And he came and stood upon the high ground. And the people cried out saying: Lord, come thou down to where the waters are to see how we suffer.

And he said: I cannot. Know ye that these boots are but a fashion item. Like ye the red toe-caps? They will not keep the water out, nay any more than I have. Besides, the keepers of beasts have the dung of their animals upon their garments and I cannot bear the smell.

Then said the people: We have paid our taxes and given our tithes so that thy labourers might dig the rivers to keep them flowing, but behold they flow not. We gave thee money for shovels, yet shovels there are none. What hast thou done with them?

Then said Lord Smith: I have sold them, for ye cannot fly in the face of nature. Behold it is written by the prophets: Wheresoever the waters desire to go, there they will go. Man is as naught against a mighty flood.

Then said the people: So what hast thou done with our taxes?

Lord Smith said: Know ye that my servants need fine raiment to clothe themselves and gilded chariots to journey in. They must wine and dine well, else they will not work. We must care for the birds of the air that they might have homes wherein to roost and raise their young. It all costs.

Then said the people: Talking about money, thou labourest but two days a week yet for each week pocketest two thousand pounds. There is one called Ian, who sitteth on the right hand of our leader, David, who saith thou shouldst no longer be rewarded thus, that thou art a waste of space, yea and a coward.

Lord Smith said: Know ye this: I have much other work to do, so can I only toil for two days a week managing the waters. Besides I shall not always be with you: before many days have passed I shall be gone from this place, my pockets well lined and my retirement well provided for. Think ye then that I really care a toss about the flooding?

Now must I depart hence, for the hour of dinner approacheth.

LEFT: DREDGING IN MOORLAND, 12TH MAY 2014
ABOVE: BURROWBRIDGE, 3RD MAY 2014

"20 years of criminal neglect – when it's all done I shiver to guess the money that it will cost to put right. They haven't got a clue. If you are going to dredge something it's all or nothing. All us old boys that have worked on the river are in agreement this is not dredging, this is lip service. It's half of what they promised last year. They call this dredging, I call it trimming the banks. It will not satisfy. If we have rains like last year we will have a problem again. I was managing director at Oswall plant services and was hired between '68 and '96 to dredge the rivers. Then the Thatcher era of privatisation came and in '89 the water authorities became privatised. In the few months before the national river authorities (later the EA) was set up to take over river maintenance, the machines of the local river board had been asset stripped and the kit sold off for scrap. It was a sick period of our lives"

CHRIS OSBOURNE, Langport Town Councillor, May 2014

LEFT: THORNEY HOUSE, 27TH FEBRUARY 2014
ABOVE: THORNEY HOUSE, 7TH MARCH 2014
OVERLEAF: THORNEY HOUSE, 27TH FEBRUARY 2014

NINE WEST

ABOVE: LOUISE SALWAY,
10TH MARCH 2014
LEFT: HOLLY BAILLE-GROHMAN,
24TH FEBRUARY 2014

"Five months on...It feels like 30 years of family life has come apart with the water and filth eating into every corner. You feel you can keep order at first, then gradually every corner of your life unravels into chaos. The feeling of impotence of being surrounded by water for 2 months unable to even start clearing up is unimaginable. It doesn't just rot your home it rots the fabric of your soul"

HOLLY BAILLE-GROHMAN, Silversmith, May 2014

MICRON MAGIC
HEPAFILTRATION
Maurice Hanssen

IGEL SLATER'S
Vinegar

PREVIOUS PAGE: A SKIP IN MOORLAND, 10TH MARCH 2014
RIGHT: THE SADLERS' MOORLAND, 5TH MARCH 2014

"The flooding of some of the villages on the Somerset Levels is devastating. No one could have predicted the despair and frustration that people feel while they try and rebuild their homes and lives now that the water has receded. Perhaps this situation would be easier to bear if it was a natural disaster or an act of God. However the flooding was totally preventable and man was totally at fault – this indeed is a bitter pill for many to swallow."

REBECCA HORSINGTON, June 2014

RIGHT: JOHNNY LEACH AT HIS WHEEL, 12TH MAY 2014
OVERLEAF: BEN LEACH STOKING THE KILN. IT WAS THE FIRST FIRING IN 6 MONTHS DUE TO FLOOD DAMAGE, 12TH MAY 2014

"I came here 50 years ago and until last year we have never been flooded. To have been flooded twice in 14 months is mind-blowing. We left the house and closed the business for 2 whole months. It took the stuffing out of us. The last firing of the kiln we had was in first week of November so it was 6 months. It's the longest time that I have been unable to throw a pot and the longest time without firing a kiln. Life stopped. We are not fully back now and its 5 months on since the floods came in. We all love the Somerset Levels it's why we are here but we have to religiously maintain them."

JOHNNY LEACH, Potter, May 2014

ABOVE: ELVERER DEREK BRISTOW, MOORLAND, 13TH MAY 2014
RIGHT: WITHY GROWER MALCOLM MUSGROVE, 12TH MAY 2014

"Years ago when I started elvering the tide used to push the elvers up to langport with the lock gates up. Now with the banks restricted with silt the tide can't push the elvers up like in the old days. It stands to reason if the water can't get up, the flood water can't get out." DEREK BRISTOW, Elverer, May 2014

"Harvesting was a huge challenge, we managed to complete 3 months work in approximately 3 weeks. The raw, unpeeled brown willow is dirty because of the flood water, but otherwise fine. All things considered it could have been much worse. We managed to harvest 80% of the crop."
NICOLA COATE, Withy Grower, May 2014

RIGHT: STARVED OWL MOORLAND, 12TH MAY 2014
OVERLEAF: THE ROAD TO HAMBRIDGE, 11TH JANUARY 2014
OVERLEAF: BURROW MUMP, 20TH JANUARY 2014

"The Somerset Levels are thought to be one of three remaining strongholds for UK Barn Owls. It is almost as though they are Barn Owl re-populating pump, adding new Owls into surrounding areas and beyond.

In 2012 we witnessed Barn Owlet production reduce dramatically due to constant rain throughout the late spring and summer. Adult Barn Owls were then forced to hunt on grassverges alongside roads due to the flooded fields. Now, in early 2014 flooded fields will have impacted on the Barn Owls and their prey once again. Some owls have perished and many moved to other areas.

How long it will take before the population can recover on the Levels remains to be seen."

CHRIS SPERRING, MBE,
Conservation Officer, Hawk and Owl Trust, May 2014

WITH THANKS

Previously I could not have imagined that I would spend two months in waders on the Levels, but it has been a remarkable experience. The community spirit and generosity of both those affected and the volunteers from across the country was a lesson in humanity.

I want to thank all the people that appear in this book and have allowed me to tell their story. A special thanks to Rebecca Horsington for being my co-conspirator, facilitator, wordsmith and editor of all things flood related; Simon de Bruxelles and James Crowden for your advice and help with text and layouts; Priscille Neefs for lending your graphic design expertise; Di Temperley, for being my constant sidekick; Stefano Broli for picture editing; Ed Stone for helping organise the story and Lara Stower for helping with design. Thank you also to those that drove, rowed, paddled, and sailed me through the water – you know who you are.

Finally, I would like to thank Mole Valley Farmers and the Bradford's Group who have sponsored this book.